I0007775

INTRODUCTION TO YAML

DEMYSTIFYING YAML DATA SERIALIZATION FORMAT

Tarun Telang

Second Edition

Introduction to YAML: Demystifying YAML data serialization format

Copyright © 2022 Tarun Telang

This work is subject to copyright. All rights are reserved by the Publisher, whether the whole or part of the material is concerned, specifically the rights of translation, reprinting, reuse of illustrations, recitation, broadcasting, reproduction on microfilms or in any other physical way, and transmission or information storage and retrieval, electronic adaptation, computer software, or by similar or dissimilar methodology now known or hereafter developed.

ISBN: 979-8-5767-2396-6

Trademarked names, logos, and images may appear in this book. Rather than use a trademark symbol with every occurrence of a trademarked name, logo, or image we use the names, logos, and images only in an editorial fashion and to the benefit of the trademark owner, with no intention of infringement of the trademark.

The use in this publication of trade names, trademarks, service marks, and similar terms, even if they are not identified as such, is not to be taken as an expression of opinion as to whether or not they are subject to proprietary rights.

While the advice and information in this book are believed to be true and accurate at the date of publication, neither the authors nor the editors nor the publisher can accept any legal responsibility for any errors or omissions that may be made. The publisher makes no warranty, express or implied, with respect to the material contained herein.

Cover designed by And Thinks Like That, Inc (https://atltinc.com/).

Cover image by Mohit Goswami

For information on translations, reprint, paperback, or audio rights please e-mail hello@taruntelang.me.

Any source code or other supplementary material referenced by the author in this book is available to readers on GitHub (https://github.com/ttelang/learn-yaml).

This book is dedicated to my grandparents, parents, wife Nikita, and son Vihan. They have always been a source of inspiration and encouragement to me. It's also for all the software and technology creators who work hard to make our planet a better place.

—Tarun Telang

Table of Contents

About the Author

 **Tarun Telang** is a hands-on technologist with extensive experience in the design and implementation of multi-tiered, highly scalable software applications. He has been part of several well-known companies such as Microsoft, Oracle, Polycom, and SAP. He has over 17 years of expertise in architecting and developing business applications.

He began his career as an enterprise Java developer at SAP, where he has developed distributed application software for big firms. He got his start with Enterprise Session Beans and Message Driven Beans, as well as instrumenting enterprise applications' configuration and management using the Java Management Extensions (JMX) technology.

He quickly mastered various enterprise technologies like Enterprise Beans, Java Management Extensions, Servlets, and Server Pages technologies, and in his first year as a developer, he became Sun Certified Programmer for the Java Platform, Standard Edition 6; and SAP Certified Development Consultant for the SAP NetWeaver Java Web Application Server (which was a Java EE 5 compliant application server).

He also gained expertise in XML technologies like XSLT and XSD. He developed several solutions using Session Beans and Message Driven Beans to handle message-oriented communications across numerous systems. In 2007, Tarun was named SAP Mentor and Community Influencer for his articles and blog posts on emerging technologies and for promoting innovative solutions in the SAP Developer Community. He frequently writes articles on Java and related technologies. Tarun has also authored multiple online courses, including a best-selling course on YAML data serialization language.

He has presented technical lectures at several developer conferences, including SAP TechEd and the Great Indian Developer Summit. For more than 15 years, he has been presenting at conferences about software technology and actively publishing technical papers and blogs to assist everyone in better grasping the fundamentals of software technology. Tarun has also developed cloud-based video conferencing applications using a microservices architecture with the Spring framework and has experience working with Persistence APIs and Hazelcast framework for building REST-based services.

Later, he led the development of many end-to-end cloud-based solutions using various architectural patterns, including Microservices and Service Oriented Architecture. Tarun has gained expertise in Web, Mobile, and Cloud technologies. He is also thorough in applied agile methodologies, including user-centric & mobile-first design for managing projects with cross-functional teams located in multiple geographies.

Having previously worked in Canada and Germany, Tarun currently resides in Hyderabad, India, with his wife and child. You can follow him on LinkedIn (https://www.linkedin.com/in/taruntelang/), Facebook (https://www.facebook.com/tarun.telang), or Twitter (@taruntelang). You can visit and like this Facebook page - "Introduction to YAML" (https://www.facebook.com/yaml_intro/) to get the latest updates. His blogs at https://blogs.taruntelang.me is an excellent resource for all things related to software technology!

I look forward to hearing from you!

Acknowledgments

I would like to thank my wife, Nikita, and son, Vihan, for their patience and love throughout the process of writing this book. I am indebted to all my mentors and friends who always encouraged me to keep on growing in every phase of my professional career.

I'd like to thank my parents for pushing me in the right direction with technology and always supporting me every step, even when I decided to do something completely different than they expected. It's also important to note that without them, I probably wouldn't have become a developer and had such a great career. Lastly, thanks again to my wife (and soulmate), Nikita. It's an incredible feeling to be with someone who keeps you motivated and challenges you not only professionally but personally as well.

Thank you for always being there for me!

Finally, I would like to thank you, the reader, for taking the time to read this book. I hope that it will help you in your journey of becoming a better software professional.

From the Author's Desk

My passion is helping beginners get started in the complex field of computer programming; therefore, my courses focus on the fundamentals and basic principles of programming.

This book has been designed to help you learn about YAML at a pace that works for your schedule. Essentially, I want to make sure that every minute you invest in mastering this topic should yield the best results possible!

Thank you for your interest in this book. Let's get started!

Preface

YAML is a very popular data format for storing configuration information and is used in almost all modern DevOps tools like Docker, Kubernetes, Ansible, and many more.

YAML is a data serialization language that allows you to represent data in an easy-to-read format. YAML's syntax is straightforward, and the language offers several features that make it robust and versatile. YAML is used by many different programming languages, and its popularity is only going to continue to grow.

Anyone looking to create structured data in a human-readable format should learn YAML. This book is aimed at software professionals of all levels, from beginner to advanced, who want to get up to date with YAML syntax.

Target Audience

This book is for Software Engineers, Full Stack Web Developers, DevOps Engineers, Software Architects, Managers, Hobbyists, or anyone wondering what YAML is.

Or anyone looking to get familiar with YAML

Figure 0-1: Target Audience for this book

It would also be helpful for someone familiar with the basics of YAML but looking to use advanced features of YAML.

Prerequisites

There are no prerequisites for this course.

However, basic knowledge and familiarity with any of the following technologies would be helpful but is not mandatory:

- HTML,
- XML,
- JSON

Objectives

After reading this book, you will be able to understand the following:

- What is YAML?
- You will become conversant with the syntax of YAML.
- You will be able to read and understand files containing YAML data.
- You will be able to create structured data in YAML data format.
- You will be able to update and maintain data using the YAML format.
- You will be able to use various data types (including complex data types of YAML.
- You will be able to use the advanced features of YAML.
- You will get an overview of the use cases where YAML is used.

You will also get to learn about various tools for creating YAML effectively.

This book provides an overview of YAML. It will go through the basic concepts behind this language and explain its main features and show the capabilities of YAML.

Every software engineer looking to create structured data in a human-readable format should learn YAML.

This book is aimed at software engineers of all levels, from beginner to advanced, who want to get up to date with YAML. It will introduce you to the YAML data serialization language and cover its syntax. It will cover basic concepts of this language, explain its main features, and show some of the key capabilities of YAML.

It will explore several YAML features that include:

- scalar data types (i.e., strings and numbers)
- containers (a list of elements)

- rich data types (i.e., dates and times)
- anchors (a way to create links in YAML documents)
- comments (provide information about the document)
- serialization (how to convert data structures to YAML format)
- document metadata (provide information about the whole document)

This book will cover these features and explain how they work together with many examples and exercises. Once you finish this book, you will have a great new skill that is transferable and highly applicable.

Introduction to YAML

This chapter will cover what YAML is all about, what other data serialization languages or formats are like YAML and its benefits.

Overview of YAML

YAML stands for *YAML Ain't Markup Language* (a recursive acronym). Its pronunciation rhymes with "camel". Figure 1-1 depicts the YAML logo. Previously, it stood for *Yet Another Markup Language*, but later it was changed to emphasize that the language is intended for data and not documents.

Figure 1-1: YAML Logo

- YAML is a very **simple**, text-based, human-readable language used to exchange data between people and computers.
- YAML is *NOT* a **programming language**. It is mainly used for storing configuration information.
- YAML files store data, and they do not include commands and instructions.
- YAML is a data serialization language like XML or JSON. However, it is much more human-readable and concise.

If you are wondering what data serialization is, here is its definition.

__Data serialization__ is converting data objects, or object states present in complex data structures into a stream of bytes for storage, transfer, and distribution in a form that can allow recovery of its original structure.

Its design is similar in structure to other markup languages, such as HTML and XML, but with specific syntax differences that enable computers to parse it quickly.

Where is YAML used?

YAML can represent any data structure that can be represented using either XML or JSON format.

YAML can be used for storing and managing any textual data in Unicode format. This makes it a software and hardware **platform independent** for storing, transporting and sharing data.

YAML is extensively used in configuration files, log files, object **persistence, caching, and messaging**. It is essential to understand this format because any changes to these files can cause your application to work incorrectly.

Below are the definitions of persistence, caching, and messaging for your reference.

Persistence is the process of preserving the state of an object longer than the lifespan or duration of the process of creating the object. This is achieved by storing the object's state in a non-volatile memory like a hard disk instead of a volatile memory like RAM.

Caching is a technique to store a copy of a resource that is requested repeatedly and serve it back from its copy itself instead of retrieving it again from the remote server. This makes the application more responsive.

Messaging is sending information across various software components or applications.

The original design of YAML was to cater to data storage. However, it has become more common for configuration files in modern software applications because it offers certain advantages over other markup languages, such as being easier to read and write by humans and having a simpler and more flexible syntax.

Whether we use it for configuration files or another purpose, YAML is a powerful and versatile language that can help to make your data more readable, organized, and maintainable.

Benefits of YAML

YAML has the following characteristics:

- **Human-readable** - YAML is very much human-readable. It allows you to represent complex data structures in a human-readable manner. To prove this point, even the homepage of the YAML's Official site (https://yaml.org) is displayed as a YAML document.
- **Simple and clean syntax:** YAML has a simple and clean syntax. It is easy to learn and simple to read. It can easily express a wide variety of different data structures.
- **Strict** - The YAML specification has very little leeway for flexibility, which increases its robustness.
- **Easy to implement and use** - It is easy to implement and use.
- **Unambiguous** - YAML unambiguously specifies the data structures of the serialized data, so there's no need to rely on comments or documentation. Because the data structures are unambiguous, it makes it easier to use automated tools (scripts) for reading and writing YAML. For example, you could write a script that reads the data structure from a file in YAML and converts it to another format (such as JSON or XML).
- **Consistent** - YAML has a consistent data model to support generic **tools. It has powerful tools, such as PyYAML.**
- **Easy to implement and use** - YAML is easy to implement and use.
- **Version control friendly** - YAML stores plain text, so it can be added to a version control such as Git or Subversion repository without any issues.
- **Fast** - YAML is fast to load and easy to process in memory.

- **Version control friendly** - YAML stores plain text, so it can be added to a version control such as Git or Subversion repository without any issues.
- **Powerful** - YAML is more potent than JSON when specifying complex data structures. It's a superset of JSON, which means that all valid JSON documents are also valid YAML.
- **Expressive and extensible** - YAML is very expressive and extensible. By extensibility, we mean existing applications continue to work even when new data is added.
- **Portable across programming languages** - YAML is portable across most of the programming languages. It supports representing sequences as lists and mappings as dictionaries (hashes in some languages) in a language-independent manner.
- **Matches native data structures** - YAML matches native data structures of modern programming languages such as Python, Ruby, and JavaScript. There are multiple YAML parsers in different languages, so you can use the same language for generating and parsing YAML.
- **Supports one-pass or one-direction processing** - Parsing YAML is linear. There are no forward or backward pointers to deal with, so there are fewer parsing ambiguities.
- **Secure** - Many security issues in programming languages are related to parsing untrusted input (such as JSON). Python, Ruby, Java, JavaScript, PHP, and more allow attackers to exploit these vulnerabilities by bypassing unexpected input strings to the parser. YAML is designed to prevent these exploits by specifying what type of data each part of the YAML stream must consist of.

Due to the above benefits, numerous modern tools and applications rely on YAML.

Understanding YAML is essential because any changes to the files that store configuration data in the YAML format can cause an application based on it to work incorrectly.

Versions

The following are different versions of the YAML language
- 1.0,
- 1.1,
- 1.2, and 1.2.2

History of YAML

- Clark Evans, Ingy döt Net, and Oren Ben-Kiki created the YAML specification in 2001. It took inspiration from existing markup languages like XML and Perl.
- In early 2004, the first official version of the YAML 1.0 specification was released.
- In 2005, the YAML 1.1 standard was released. By this time, JSON had become widespread. Accidentally JSON was a subset of YAML (both syntactically and semantically).
- YAML 1.2 was released in 2009 to ensure it is a valid superset of JSON. YAML 1.2 has been updated to include more security features, making it more resistant to attacks.
- YAML 1.2.2 is the latest revision of the YAML specification. It was released on 1st October 2021. It mainly focuses on improving clarity, readability and removing ambiguity in the specification.
- Various applications and software projects have used YAML over the years. Some notable examples include Ansible, Ruby on Rails, and Drupal.

Summary

- YAML stands for YAML Ain't Markup Language.
- YAML is a very simple text-based data format for exchanging data
- It is like XML or JSON.
- YAML files usually store configuration data.
- YAML is a human-readable, clean, simple, easy to implement, consistent, portable, expressive, and extensible data serialization format.

## CHAPTER 2

YAML Syntax

In this chapter, you will learn about the basic syntax of the YAML language. You will learn about adding comments in YAML and creating a single YAML file or stream with multiple documents.

YAML Basics

Let us now learn the basics of YAML syntax; as you know, YAML is a text-based format. It is a simple format so this example below, which lists the learning objective, is also a valid YAML.

Example

Below is a basic example of a YAML file:

```
---
- Title: "Learn YAML from Scratch"
- Message: "Welcome to this course"
- Learning Objectives:
    - "What is YAML?"
    - "Basic Syntax"
    - "Data Types"
    - "Using Complex data types"
    - "Advance features and capabilities"
    - "Tools and Technologies leveraging
YAML"
    - "Creating and Validating YAML Data"
```

Below is the visual representation of the above list for your better understanding.

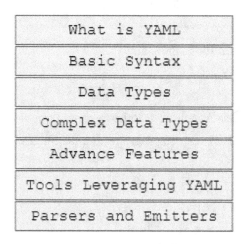

Figure 2-1: *List of Learning Objectives*

In C-based programming language, this would have been represented programmatically as the code snippet below:

Example

```
LearningObjectives[0] = "What is YAML?"
LearningObjectives[1] = "Basic Syntax"
LearningObjectives[2] = "Data Types"
LearningObjectives[3] = "Complex Data Types"
LearningObjectives[4] = "Advance Features"
LearningObjectives[5] = "Tools Leveraging YAML"
LearningObjectives[6] = " Parsers and Emitters"
```

As you can see, YAML files are straightforward to read and understand. They are also relatively concise, which makes them ideal for storing and organizing large amounts of data.

YAML is worth considering if you're looking for a simple and efficient way to store and manage your data. Many excellent libraries and tools are available for working with YAML, so it's easy to get started.

Some of the most popular libraries for working with YAML include:
- YamlDotNet for .NET,
- PyYaml for Python, and
- SnakeYaml for Java.

You can refer to Appendix B to learn about popular libraries for emitting and parsing YAML in various programming languages.

Key-value pairs

YAML is very much human-readable. YAML is a clean format because all the data is represented as a key-value pair. A **key-value pair** is a simple data structure that consists of a unique identifier (the key) and the corresponding value of that identifier.

The key can be any data type, such as a text string or an integer.
The value can also be of any type of data,
including string, integer, float, boolean, list, or key-value pairs.

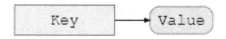

Figure 2-2: Key-value pair

Key-value pairs are represented using the following syntax.

Syntax

```
<key>: <value>
```

where <key> represents key name and <value> represents data separated by colon (:). The whitespace after the colon is mandatory.

Example #1

```
- Title: "Learn YAML from Scratch"
```

Let's say we have the data as shown below:

Name	Age	Occupation
John Doe	43	Software Engineer

Table 2-1: *Employee Data*

Example #2

We can represent this in YAML using key-value pairs as follows:

```
name: John Doe
age: 43
occupation: Software Engineer
```

Here you have a key Title on the left, then a colon, and then single whitespace. A value may contain any data type; in this case, it is a string or text.

The whitespace is very important; without this, the YAML will be invalid. For a text or a string, you may use quotation marks, a single quote (') or a double quote ("), or no quotes at all.

Quotes are optional. However, they are mainly used to prevent misinterpretation from a parser working on the YAML data so that it does not get converted to another data type or if we want to include special characters or whitespace.

In YAML, we use whitespaces for defining the structure. Whitespaces provide structure to the document. E.g., in the example above, Learning

Objectives is the parent, then there is an indentation with two whitespaces followed by various objective items as its children.

You should always be careful that you use only white spaces, and in case you accidentally add tabs, the YAML will become invalid.

Uses of a key-value pair

Here are some of the most common uses of key-value pairs:
- They are used in the implementation of hash tables, whereby they are used to store and retrieve information.
- Many programming languages include built-in support for key-value pairs as a core data structure, making them a fundamental part of many software applications.

Key-value pairs provide a powerful and flexible way to store and work with data.

List

A list is represented by preceding its items with - (hyphen). It's an **ordered collection** of data.

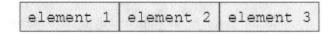

Figure 2-3: list or sequence

Syntax

```
- <element 1>
- <element 2>
```

```
  - ...
  - <element n>
```

YAML is case-sensitive.

Example

```
- DATA
- data
- Key: data
- KEY: DATA
```

The following is the graphical representation of the sample YAML data in the code example above:

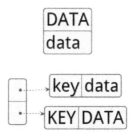

Figure 2-4: Graphical representation of sample YAML data

All these values in the example above are unique, they are not duplicates, and they will be treated as distinct values by YAML.

Figure 2-4: YAML *is case sensitive*

YAML structures are determined by indentations like that of the Python programming language.

Spaces are the only way to achieve indentation. Tabs are not allowed in YAML.

Tip: Enable displaying whitespace characters in your text editor to prevent accidental use of tabs of additional spacings.

Simple yet Powerful

It's simple syntax does not limit its language capabilities. The language is rich enough to represent almost any conceivable data structure or object inside a running computer program as a readable plain text file.

Later in this book, we will see the features of YAML that make it an excellent option for data representation.

Multi-Document Support in YAML

To define a YAML file, we use *.yml* or *.yaml* extensions, e.g. *config.yml*.

You can add multiple documents to a single YAML file.

We begin a YAML document with three hyphens (---). This is optional.

A YAML file is a stream of data containing multiple documents. As in the case of the example mentioned below, there are two documents, and each of them is started with three hyphens (---).

YAML is case sensitive, so these are all unique values, they are not duplicates, and they will be treated as distinct values by YAML.

When you end a document, you again use three hyphens (---), but there is an exception to this rule if you have the last document. In that case, you use three dots (. . .). Three dots (. . .) represents the end of a document without starting a new document, so it represents the end of the stream.

Different documents are separated using three dashes (---). Use three dots (. . .) to mark the end of a document without starting a new one.

Let's look at the example below to understand this better.

Example

```
---
 - XML
 - JSON
 - CSV
---
 - Unicode
 - ASCII
 - UTF8
. . .
```

Below is the graphical representation of the above YAML stream.

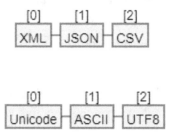

Figure 2-5: Visualization of the multi-document data stream

YAML stream is a collection of zero or more documents. An empty stream contains no documents. Documents may optionally end with (...). A single document may or may not be marked with (---).

Block Style

Block style is a way of formatting YAML documents typically used to represent hierarchical data structures. In block style, each document element is wholly contained within its block element. This allows flexibility and control when working with large or complex data structures. Individual elements can be easily referenced, modified, or removed without affecting the rest of the document.

A document in block style uses spaces for structuring the document. It is very much human-readable but is less compact. One common way to format a YAML document in block style is by starting with a top-level root element and then indenting all child elements from that level.

Example #1

For example, here is a simple "hello world" program represented using this convention:

```
---
hello: world
...
```

In the above code, (---) denotes the start of a new document, whereas (. . .) denotes the end of the document.

Example #2

```
color:
   - red
   - yellow
   - blue
```

Below is the graphical representation of the data:

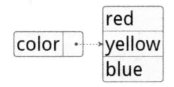

Figure 2-6: Visualization of the YAML data

Example #3

```
---
# list of markup languages
Formats:
- XML: eXtensible Markup Language,
- JSON: JavaScript Object Notation,
- CSV: Comma-separated Values
---
# list of encodings
Encodings:
   - Unicode
```

```
 - ASCII
 - UTF8
---
# list of programming languages
Language:
 - Java
 - C++
 - Python
...
```

To represent nested data structures, simply continue indenting child elements from their parent element. For example, below is a more complex data structure that contains a list of user information:

Example #4

```
---
users:
  - name: John Smith
    age: 25
    job: programmer
  - name: Jane Doe
    age: 30
    job: manager
...
```

Block style allows us to represent hierarchical data structures simply, making it an ideal choice for working with large or complex data.
The above style, where hyphens (–) and spaces ( ) are used to specify a list of items, is known as Block Style.

Flow style

YAML has an alternate syntax called **flow style**; it allows *sequences* and *mappings* to be written inline without relying on indentation, using a pair of square brackets [ ] and curly brackets { } respectively.

It was introduced as an alternative to the more common block style, which involves arranging YAML elements into separate blocks based on their level in the data hierarchy. In contrast, the flow style uses a single line for each element and places them directly next to each other. This can make for a more concise and readable YAML, especially when dealing with simple data structures.

Flow style is an extension of JSON. It is less human readable however provides more compactness. The flow style syntax begins with a left curly brace ({), followed by the data structure elements separated by commas (,).

Each element must be on its line, without any indentation. The last element must also be followed by a right curly brace (}). Below is an example of a basic flow style YAML document:

Below is an example of a basic flow style YAML document:

```
{ element1, element2, element3}
```

Example #1

```
color: [red, blue]
```

Example #2

```
- { name: 'James', age: 35 }
```

Example #3

```
---
# list of markup languages
Formats: [{ "XML": "eXtensible Markup Language"
}, {
"JSON": "JavaScript Object Notation" }, {"CSV":
```

```
 "Comma-separated Values"}]
---
# list of encodings
Encodings: [ Unicode, ASCII, UTF8]
---
# list of programming
Languages: [Java, C++, Ruby]
...
```

Flow style lets us write data in one line. We use commas to separate the data. The left curly brace marks the start of the data structure, and the right curly brace marks the ends of it. We can also nest data inside other data structures.

Example# 4

```
{ "key": "value",
  "array": ["element1", "element2"],
  "nested object": { "subkey1": "subvalue1",
"subkey2": "subvalue2" }
}
```

The above code uses inline JSON to represent lists and key-value pairs. This also makes YAML a superset of JSON.

As flow style is more concise than block style, it is often preferred by developers who need to write complex or lengthy data structures. Additionally, using the flow style can reduce the chances of errors due to indention since there is no need to keep track of indentation levels.

Flow style is a valuable syntax for describing data structures in YAML. Whether we're working with simple or complex data, it can help make our code more readable and easier to understand by using a single line per element. However, it can also be more challenging to work with than block style if our data contains many nested elements or complex structures.

Regardless, it is an essential format for developers who work with YAML regularly.

Benefits

As flow style is more concise than block style and produces cleaner code, it is often preferred by developers who need to write complex or lengthy data structures. Additionally, using the flow style can reduce the chances of errors due to indention since there is no need to keep track of indentation levels.

Comments

To write effective YAML code, it is crucial to understand how to use comments effectively. This involves understanding the syntax for adding comments and knowing when and where to use them.

Syntax

Any text after # not enclosed in ' ' (quotes) or " " (double quotes) is considered as comments. It marks the beginning of a comment, and any text until the end of the line is completely ignored. You use this to write notes on the file or temporarily disable some sections of this file.

Below are some examples of the comments.

Example #1

```
# A single-line comments
```

To create a multi-line, you must suffix each line with a # character.

A comment can begin from anywhere in the line.

Example #2

```
# Document starts below
---
key: "value" # mapping
    # A list of two items
list:
  - "item 1" # first value
  - "item 2" # second value
---
# end of the document
```

To create a multi-line, you must suffix each line with a # character.

Example #3

```
# This is a multi-line
# comment in YAML. There is
# no alternate way of creating
# block comments.
```

Note: YAML does not support block or multi-line comments.

Below is another example of YAML comments:

Example #4

The hash # marks the beginning of the comment, and any text until the end of the line is considered part of the comment. Hence, it is entirely ignored by YAML parsers.

When and where to use comments

Generally, it's a good idea to use comments sparingly and only when necessary. Adding too many comments can make the code more difficult to read and understand. In most cases, it's best to add comments where the code is complex or convoluted or where there is a need to provide additional instructions on using certain features.

Additionally, we should avoid using comments to duplicate information already provided in the documentation or existing comments.

Using effective comments in YAML can help make our code more readable and easier to understand for other programmers. To become skilled in YAML, it's essential to understand the syntax for adding comments and when and where to use them. By following these tips mentioned above, we can write code that is both clean and well-documented.

Summary

- Items of a list in YAML are represented by preceding it with - (hyphen).
- Key value pairs in YAML are represented as <key>:<value>.
- YAML is **case-sensitive**.
- To define a YAML file we use either *.yml* or *.yaml* extensions
- Different documents in YAML can be separated using three dashes (---).
- You use three dots (...) to mark the **end of a document** without starting a new one.
- A document in **block style** uses spaces for structuring the document.
- **Flow style** makes YAML an extension of JSON. It is a little less human-readable but provides more compactness to the document.

- Any text after # not enclosed in "(quotes) or "" (double quotes) is considered as comments.
- YAML does not support block or multi-line comments.

## CHAPTER 3

Data Types in YAML

In this chapter, you learn about various data types available in YAML and how to represent them.

Data Types

YAML supports all data types of agile languages such as Perl, Python, PHP, Ruby, and JavaScript. Following is the list of supported data types:

- Boolean
- Numbers
- Strings
- Dates
- Timestamp
- Arrays
- Maps
- Nulls

Variable (Scalars)

A name followed by a colon (:) and a single space (   ) defines a variable (also known as scalars). Scalars are the simplest data type in YAML and can represent basic types, including boolean, integers, and floating-point numbers.

See the example below about how to represent a string, an integer, a floating-point number, and a boolean value in YAML:

Example

```
string: "Hello"
integer: 123
float: 12.345
boolean: No
```

Below is the graphical representation of the example above:

string	Hello
integer	123
float	12.345
boolean	No

Figure 3-1: Graphical visualization of YAML code

As we can see, the format for each data type is very similar.

To represent a string in YAML, we use a single quote (') or a double quote (") and the actual string value within these quotes. We use the standard numeric literals for integers and floating-point numbers. Boolean values can be represented in YAML using the keywords like true and false or Yes and No.

Specifying Data Types Explicitly using Tags

YAML can autodetect types. However, it is often necessary to explicitly specify the type using a tag. To force a type, we can prefix the type with a !! symbol. Here's an example:

Example

```
age: !!float 23
married: !!str true
```

```
binary: !!int 0b101010
hexadecimal: !!int 0x1C7A
name: !!str "James"
```

Here is the table showing a list of tags supported in YAML along with its
description

Tag	Description
!!bool	Denotes a boolean value
!!int	Denotes a integer value
!!float	Denotes a floating point number
!!str	Denotes a string

Table 3-1: Common tags supported in YAML

Integers

Integers represent arbitrary-sized finite mathematical integers.

Example

```
---
negative: !!int -12
zero: !!int 0
positive: !!int 23
binary: 0b101010
octal: 01672
hexadecimal: 0x1C7A
number: +687_456
sexagesimal: 180:30:20 # base 60
```

A number can be written in **binary** form by prefixing it with *0b* or *0B*. Here
you can use the 0 and 1 digits only. **Octal** literals are written with a leading 0
(zero). Only the digits 0 through 7 are used. **Hexadecimal** literals use *0x* or
0X as a prefix and use the digits 0 through 9 and then *A (or a)* through *F (or
f)* for values 10 through 15.

Floating Point

It represents an approximation to real numbers, including three special values (positive and negative infinity and "not a number").

Example

```
negative: !!float -1.23
zero: !!float 0.0
positive: !!float 2.3e4
infinity: !!float .inf
not a number: !!float .nan
```

Here *.inf* represents infinity, and *.nan* represents Not a Number. Interestingly, both of these are considered to be floating point values in YAML.

Boolean

Boolean represents a true/false value.

Example

```
---
married: !!bool true
odd: !!bool false
```

In addition to true/false, you may also use the following use for denoting boolean values:

- True/False,
- ON/OFF,
- Yes/No
- y/n

String

Strings are a series of characters, usually represented by letters, numbers, and symbols. They're used to communicate information in textual form. It represents a Unicode string, a sequence of zero or more Unicode characters.

If we want to represent a string with quotes, we can use either single or double-quotes. For example, both of the following are valid representations of the string "hello world":

Example #1

```
# single-quoted string
'hello world'

# double-quoted string
"hello world"
```

If we want to represent a string without quotes, we can use the unquoted style. This is how we can represent the same string, "hello world", without using any quotes:

Example #2

```
# unquoted string
hello world
```

Example #2

```
---
name: !!str "James"
message: !!str "This is a \n multiline text"
```

In YAML, escape sequences can be used within double quotes to represent non-printable characters. YAML escape sequences are a superset of C's escape sequences. If we want to represent a string with quotes, we can use either single or double quotes. If we want to represent a string without quotes, we can use the unquoted style.

The following are a few rules to follow when using the unquoted style:
1. The string can only contain alphanumeric characters and hyphens.
2. The string cannot start with a number or punctuation character.
3. The string cannot be a keyword in YAML.

Representing strings in YAML

In YAML, strings can be represented in the following several ways:

- Single-quoted scalars
- Double-quoted scalars
- Unquoted scalars
- Folded scalars
- Literal scalars

Let's look into each of these ways of representing strings in detail.

Below is an example to demonstrate the different ways of representing Strings in 'YAML.'

Single-quoted scalars

A **single-quoted scalar** is a basic string with any character except for the single quote ('). They cannot span multiple lines.

These are useful when we need to represent special characters in our strings. The example of single-quoted scalars is as follows:

Example #2

```
text: Hello
quoted:
  - 'single quoted string'
  - "double quoted strings"
```

A | character denotes a string with newlines preserved.

Example #3

```
text: |
  Every line in this text
  will be stored
  as separate lines.
```

A > character denotes a string with newlines folded.

Example #4

```
text: >
  This text will
  be wrapped into
  a single paragraph
```

Strings can be written simply **without** quotes or enclosed within a pair of ' single or " double quotation symbols.

Note: When the value is text, you use quotes to make sure any special characters are not given any special meaning. Although they are optional, their use is highly recommended.

In YAML, strings can be represented in the following several ways:
- Single-quoted scalars
- Double-quoted scalars
- Unquoted scalars
- Folded scalars
- Literal scalars

Let's look into each of these ways of representing strings in detail.

Single-quoted scalars

A **single-quoted scalar** is a basic string with any character except for the single quote ('). They cannot span multiple lines.

These are useful when we need to represent special characters in our strings.

Example

The example of single-quoted scalars is as follows:

```
'I\'m a YAML string!'
'I am a YAML string!'
```

Double-quoted string

A **double-quoted scalar** is a more sophisticated string that can have any character, span multiple lines, and use special characters such as the backslash (\).

These are useful when representing special characters in our strings.

Example

The example of double-quoted scalars is as follows:

```
"I'm a YAML string!"
```

Unquoted scalars

An **unquoted scalar** is a simple string that can have any character except for the following:

- Special characters: ({ } , : [] & * ? | - > ' " % @ `)
- The space character: ( )
- The tab character: (\t)
- The line feed character: (\n)
- The carriage return character: (\r)
- The null character: (\0)
- The Unicode non-breaking space character: (\u00A0)

Unquoted scalars cannot span multiple lines. These are useful when representing data that does not require any special characters.

Example

```
I'm a YAML string!
```

Literal scalars

The | character is used to denote literal scalars, which are strings that preserve all whitespace and line breaks. The | character indicates that the following lines are part of the string until a blank line is reached.

Example

An example of literal scalars is as follows:

```
| This is a literal string
  spanning multiple lines.
```

Representing strings in YAML as literal scalars

The |+ character denotes a non-specific tag for a string that preserves all newlines and leading/trailing whitespace.

The |- character denotes a non-specific tag for a string that removes all trailing empty lines and spaces and leads spaces up to the first non-empty line.

Null

Null values represent unknown, undefined values or lack of value. You can also use tilde ~, null in lowercase, NULL in uppercase, or Null in camelCase.

Null values are sometimes called nil values. However, in YAML, the term nil represents an explicit absence of a value rather than an unknown or undefined value.

Example

```
---
manager: !!null null
blank:
tilde: ~
title: null
~: null key
```

There are several ways to represent null values in YAML.
- The most common way is to use the null keyword;
- you can also use the tilde ~ character for a null value.
- Empty values are also considered to be null values.

Uses of null values

Null values can be used in various ways, depending on the context. They can be used to represent the following:

- **Unknown or undefined values:** When the value of a data element is unknown or undefined, `null` can be used as its value.

- **Empty values:** `null` can represent an empty value, such as an empty list or an empty string.

- **Placeholder values:** `null` can be used as a placeholder value when the actual value is not yet known.

- **Missing or incomplete data:** `null` values can be used to represent data that is missing or incomplete.

- **Default values for fields or parameters:** `null` values are often used with optional parameters. For example, a parameter may be specified as optional with a default value of `null`. If the parameter is not specified, the null value will be used.

- **Invalid data:** If data is invalid, `null` values can be used to represent this.

Null values are an essential part of YAML. They provide a way to represent unknown or undefined values and can be used in various ways depending on the context. When using `null` values, it is vital to know how they can be represented. This ensures that our data is correctly interpreted by others.

Timestamps

A Timestamp represents a single point in time. It uses notation from the ISO8601 format. If no time zone is added, it is assumed to be UTC. To depict the date format, you can omit the time part.

In such a case, the time defaults to 00:00:00Z.

Example

```
---
time: 2020-12-07T01:02:59:34.02Z
timestamp: 2020-12-07T01:02:59:34.02 +05:30
datetime: 2020-12-07T01:02:59:34.02+05:30
notimezone: 2020-12-07T01:02:59:34.02
date: 2020-12-07
```

Arrays

Arrays are available in almost all programming languages, including Perl, Python, PHP, Java, C#, Ruby, and JavaScript. They are linear data types used to represent a list of items.

In YAML data serialization format, you can represent arrays using two different styles, as explained below.

Block sequence

The block sequence style of YAML uses hyphens or dashes to (-) to represent arrays. A hyphen (-) followed by white space ( ) represents an element of an array. When you enter the dashes, you need to ensure that all items are at the same indentation level.

See the code example below to understand this better.

Example

```
colors:
  - red
  - green
```

```
 - blue
 - orange
```

Below is the graphical representation of the above YAML block sequence:

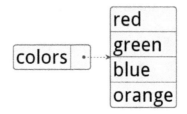

Figure 3-2: Graphical visualization of YAML code

Flow sequence

The flow sequence style of YAML uses brackets and commas to represent arrays.

See the code example below to understand this better.

Example

```
colors: [red, green, blue, orange]
```

Summary

Here is the list of supported scalar types in YAML.

Type	Description
~, null, Null	null values
1234	decimal
0b101010	binary (base 64 encoding)
0x12AD	hexadecimal
02677	octal
.inf, -.Inf	infinity
.NAN	not a number
y, Y, true, True, TRUE	true
n, N, false, False, FALSE	false
2020-12-07	date or timestamps
123_456.78	floating point or decimal numbers
123.45e+78	exponential numbers

Table 3-2: Common tags supported in YAML

YAML is a very versatile data serialization standard that can be used to represent many different data types. In this chapter, we learned to represent some of the most common data types in YAML.

Advance Data Types

Below are a few important data structures commonly seen in YAML:

- sequences (!!seq)
- ordered map (!!omap)
- set (!!set)
- pairs (!!pairs)
- maps (!!map)
- dictionaries

You will learn more about these advanced data types in the following sections.

Sequence or Array (!!seq)

A sequence is a linear data structure that represents a collection of elements. The elements in the sequence are accessed one after another.

It represents a collection indexed by sequential integers starting with zero. It is specified by placing each member on a new line with a hyphen or dash character '-'.

Example #1

For example, the following is how a list of colors can be represented:

```
- red
- green
- blue
- orange
```

or

```
colors: !!seq # Ordered sequence of nodes
  - red
  - orange
  - yellow
```

There is also a compact notation using [] for sequence. Here we represent a sequence using the start and end indicators ([and]).

Example #2

The above sequence can also be represented as below:

```
[red, green, blue, orange]
```

Below is the graphical representation of the YAML sequence:

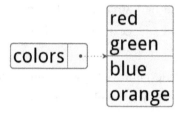

Figure 3-3: *Graphical visualization of YAML code*

Sparse sequence

A sequence where not all the keys have values is known as a sparse sequence.

Example

```
---
- ~
- blue
-
- Null
- NULL
- orange
```

The following is a graphical representation of the sparse sequence in the code example:

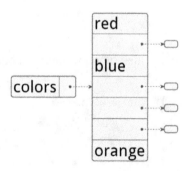

Figure 3-4: *Graphical visualization of the sparse sequence*

Nested Sequence

A **nested sequence** is a sequence that is contained within another sequence. We can also use nested sequences to represent more complex data structures.

It represents a sequence of items and sub-items. It is specified by placing a single space for each dash in the sub-items. YAML uses spaces, NOT tabs for indentation.

Example #1

For example, the following is how a list of people with their hobbies can be represented:

```
-
  name: John
  hobbies: ['sports', 'music']
-
  name: Jane
  hobbies: ['movies', 'cooking']
-
  name: Mark
  hobbies: ['tennis', 'swimming']
```

In the above example, each person has a list of hobbies. This is represented using a nested sequence.

Example #2

```
---
-
  - red
  - green
  - blue
-
```

- orange
- yellow
- brown

Mappings (!!map)

Mappings are used for storing a name-value pair. They are mainly used for setting up data in configuration parameters.

There are two ways to represent maps in YAML:
- Mapping nodes
- Mapping scalars

Mapping nodes represent complex data structures, such as hashes or dictionaries. In a mapping node, each key must be unique, and each key can have only one value. The order of the keys is not essential.

Mapping scalars represent simple data structures, such as arrays or tuples. Each key must be unique in a mapping scalar but can have multiple values. The order of the keys is essential.

Syntax

```
<name>: <value>
```

Example

```
color: red
```

Maps are represented using the colon (:) character. We can also use quotation marks (" or ') to enclose the keys and values if necessary.

We can use mapping nodes or mapping scalars to represent a map in YAML. In most cases, it is recommended to use mapping nodes. However, if we need to preserve the order of the keys, then we should use mapping scalars.

Nested Mappings

A value in a mapping can be nested inside another mapping. There is also a compact notation using {} for maps.

Example #1

```
---
# Unordered set of name: value pairs.
a: 1
b:
  c: 3
  d: 4
```

The following is a graphical representation of the nested mappings in the code example:

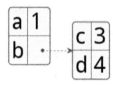

Figure 3-4: Graphical visualization of the nested mappings

As indentation is vital in YAML. The nested map must be indented further than the parent map. The above block style is equivalent to the example below:

Example #2

```
---
a: 1
b: {c: 3, d: 4}
```

The following code snippet shows how to represent employee data using maps in YAML:

Example #3

```
---
name: John Smith
age: 25
address:
  street: 123 Main Street
  city: New York
  state: NY
  zip: 10001
...
```

In the example above, the first key is name, and the value is John Smith. The second key is age, and the value is 25. The third key is the address, and the value is a nested map with four keys and four values. The fourth key is zip, and the value is 10001.

Pairs (`!!pairs`)

Pairs are an **ordered list of named values**, allowing duplicates. Many programming languages do not have pairs as a native data type; hence an application may interpret `!!pairs` as an array of hash tables containing one key each.

See the example below to understand its usage.

Example

```
# Explicitly typed pairs.
Block tasks: !!pairs
  - meeting: standup
  - meeting: demo
  - break: lunch
  - meeting: all hands
Flow tasks: !!pairs [meeting: standup, meeting:
lunch]
```

Set (!!set)

A set is an **unordered collection of nodes with distinct values**. See the example below to understand its usage.

Example

```
# Explicitly typed set.
players: !!set
  ? Mark
  ? Steve
  ? Smith

# Flow style
soccer teams: !!set {Chelsea, Arsenal,
Liverpool}
```

Dictionary (!!omap)

Dictionaries are a standard data structure in many programming languages. A dictionary is a data structure that allows us to store data in key-value pairs. In YAML, dictionaries are represented as mappings.

A **mapping** is a collection of key-value pairs, where each key is mapped to a value. A value in a mapping can be a sequence. A mapping can contain any assortment of mappings and sequences as values.

List members are denoted by a leading hyphen (-). It should be separated from the node with white space.

Example

```
Fruits: !!omap # Explicitly typed ordered map
  - Apple:
      calories: 120
      fat: 0.2 g
      carbs: 35 g
  - Banana:
      calories: 105
      fat: 0.4 g
      carbs: 27 g
```

Here is the graphical representation of the above YAML data

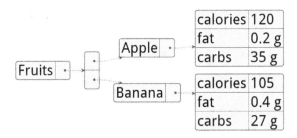

Figure 3-5: Graphical visualization of the nested mappings

Now consider the following graphical representation of a dictionary that maps several countries to their capital cities.

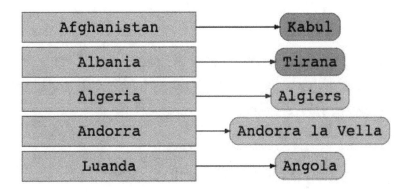

Figure: A dictionary that maps countries to their capital cities

In the example above, the countries mapping contains five key-value pairs. The keys are on the left, and the values are on the right. The keys are "Afghanistan", "Albania", "Algeria", "Andorra", and "Angola," and their corresponding values are "Kabul", "Tirana", "Algiers", "Andorra la Vella", and "Luanda," respectively. When we want to represent a dictionary in YAML, we can use either block-style or flow-style notation.

Representing dictionaries in block-style

The following is the YAML code for the above mapping represented in block-style notation:

Example

```
---
countries:
  Afghanistan: Kabul
  Albania: Tirana
  Algeria: Algiers
  Andorra: Andorra la Vella
  "Angola": "Luanda"
```

As we can see, in **block-style notation,** each key is separated from its value by a colon (:) followed by a space. We can also use quotation marks around the key or value strings, as in line 7 above.

Representing dictionaries in flow-style

We can also represent mappings in flow-style notation. The following is an equivalent YAML code to define the mapping above in flow-style notation:

Example

```
countries: {Afghanistan: Kabul, Albania:
Tirana, Algeria: Algiers, Andorra: Andorra la
Vella, "Angola": "Luanda"}
```

In flow-style notation, all key-value pairs are represented on a single line. As we can see, the dictionary is defined as a sequence of key-value pairs. We use the mapping start token ({) and the mapping end token (}) to map the key-value pairs in flow-style representation. These are used to indicate the beginning and the end of mapping, respectively.

Each key is separated from its value by a colon (:) followed by a space. Commas separate the key-value pairs (,).

Flow-style notation is more compact than block-style notation. However, it can be more challenging to read. Therefore, it is generally advisable to use block-style notation for mappings that contain more than a few key-value pairs.

## CHAPTER 4

Special Features

Anchors

Anchors are used for reusing properties. To denote references & an ampersand character is used, and an alias is represented using the * (star or asterisk) character.

Syntax

```
anchored_value: &anchorName value
other_property: *anchorName #value
```

Example

```
Strawberry:
  color: *red [255, 0, 0]
Apple:
  color: &red
```

In the above YAML code, the color property of Apple is specified as a reference to the color property of Strawberry. Here, Apple inherits the color property of Strawberry.

Merge

The << symbol indicates that all the keys of one or more specified maps should be inserted into the current map.

Example

```
parent: &base
  name: 'James'
  age: 35

employee:
  <<: *base
  married: true
```

Here employee would also have properties as below:

Example

```
name: 'James'
age: 35
```

We can also override some values (e.g., name) as below:

Example

```
<<: *base
name: 'Smith
```

This would be equivalent to

Example

```
name: 'Smith'
age: 35
```

Default Value Mapping

YAML allows users to specify default value mapping as below:

Example

```
# Default
=: 1
```

Summary

See the example YAML document below as a reference to summarize about various data types we have learned so far.

Example

```
color: "red" # String with double quotes
name: 'John' # String with single quotes
age: 32 # Integer
pi: 3.14 # Decimal
salary: 1.2345e3 # Decimal in Scientific
Notation
married: false # Boolean
date: 2010-09-08 # ISO 8601
spouse: null # Null value
description: >
  Welcome to the world of data types,
  This text would be rendered in a single
  Line.
signature: |
  Tarun
  Instructor
  email: someone@email.com
```

## CHAPTER 5

Comparison of Data Formats

In this chapter, let's use a simple document with the structure shown in Figure 9 containing employee data and its corresponding representation using all the popular data formats like XML and JSON.

This will help you further strengthen your understanding based-on on your earlier experience. You would also better understand the key differences in these data representation specifications.

Various Data Formats

Let's compare a sample dataset in XML, JSON, and YAML format.

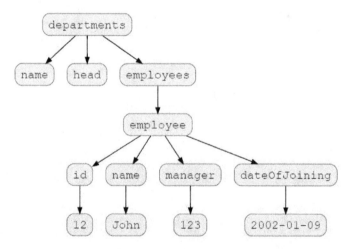

Figure 5-1: Data Model

XML

XML stands for Extensible Markup Language. It is designed to store and transport data across many different IT systems. It is heavily used for communication across multiple distributed systems over the Internet.

Example

```
<?xml version="1.0" encoding="UTF-8"?>
<Departments>
  <name>HR</name>
  <head>Director</head>
  <Employees>
    <id>12</id>
    <name>John</name>
    <manager>123434</manager>
    <dateOfJoining>2002-01-
09T00:00:00.000Z</dateOfJoining>
  </Employees>
</Departments>
```

XML is not easily readable by humans.

XML must be parsed with an **XML parser** for consuming it programmatically.

However, XML uses a lot of self-describing syntaxes.

In XML, the first line contains a prologue that defines the XML version and the character encoding as below:

```
<?xml version="1.0" encoding="UTF-8"?>
```

Next, we have the root element of the document

```
<Organization>
```

Starting from the 3rd line in the example, we have an <Department> element with properties name and head.

```
<Department name="HR" head="Director">
```

The <Employee> elements have 4 child elements namely <id>, <name>, <manager>, and <joining> represented as below

```
<id>12</id>
<name>John</name>
<manager>123</manager>
<joining>2002-01-09</joining>
```

The last line ends the element with the closing tag.

```
</Department>
```

JSON

JSON stands for *JavaScript Object Notation.* JSON is the most popular text-based data serialization format. Converting data to or from the JSON format is programmatically straightforward using JavaScript. JSON provides the lowest standard denominator information model, ensuring every modern programming language can quickly process JSON data. However, it does have some drawbacks, like manually editing JSON files is more complex than YAML.

The details of the JSON format are beyond the scope of this book. It's a straightforward format. If you are interested in further information, refer to the JSON Data Interchange Standard specification.

Example

```
{
  "Departments": [
    {
      "name": "HR",
      "head": "Director",
      "Employees": [
        {
          "id": 12,
          "name": "John",
          "manager": 123434,
          "dateOfJoining": "2002-01-
09T00:00:00.000Z"
        }
      ]
    }
  ]
}
```

JSON is a straightforward format. Data within JSON is stored in **name/value pairs** separated by commas (,).

Curly braces ({}) are used to enclose **objects**, and values enclosed within square brackets ([]) represent **arrays**.

JSON does not require special parsers as a standard JavaScript function can parse it.

YAML

YAML stands for YAML *Ain't Markup Language*. YAML's foremost design goal was to support human readability.

It can support the serialization of arbitrary native data structures. It can be integrated into applications developed using modern programming languages like Java, Python, Ruby, C#, etc.

It is more complex to generate and parse than JSON or XML.

It also provides a complete information model with more complex data types.

As YAML is a superset of JSON, it is easy to migrate from JSON to YAML to support additional features.

The YAML specification is much larger than JSON as it contains more data types and features.

Example

```
---
Departments:
  -
    name: "HR"
```

```
head: "Director"
Employees:
    -
        id: 12,
        name: "John"
        manager: 123434
        dateOfJoining: 2001-13-09
```

As you can see, YAML is a cleaner and more readable data format.

Please find some more examples of YAML data below:

Example

```
---
employee:
  id: 12
  name: smith
  salary: 10000
  address:
    city: Toronto
    state: Ontario
    country: Canada
    zip: A2NY1J
  commission:
    -
        quarter: Q1 2020
        amount: 1000
    -
        quarter: Q2 2020
        amount: 1000
```

We are adding another employee to the above sample document to demonstrate the usage of a list of dictionaries and dictionaries within a dictionary.

Example

```yaml
---
employee:
  -
    id: 12
    name: Smith
    salary: 10000
    address:
      city: Toronto
      state: Ontario
      country: Canada
      zip: A2NY1J
    commission:
      -
        quarter: Q1 2020
        amount: 1000
      -
        quarter: Q2 2020
        amount: 1000
  -
    id: 12
    name: James
    salary: 10000
    address:
      city: Seattle
      state: Washington
      country: united states
      zip: 32001
    commission:
      -
        quarter: Q1 2020
        amount: 500
      -
        quarter: Q2 2020
        amount: 700
```

APPENDIX A

Popular Tools using YAML

Below are some of the tools which are extensively leveraging the YAML data format.

and many more...

Figure A-1: Popular YAML Tools

CircleCI

CircleCI is a modern Continuous Integration and Deployment (CI/CD) tool for the cloud which can be used to automate software builds, tests, and deployment.

CircleCI uses a YAML file called *config.yml* to store its configuration. Suppose you are planning to learn or use CircleCI in your project. The concepts covered in this course are fundamental as most of the time, you would be working on this YAML file to configure CircleCI to work with your project.

Travis CI

Travis CI is a hosted continuous integration service used to build and test software projects hosted at GitHub and Bitbucket.

Travis CI uses a YAML file named .travis.yml to store its configuration in your repository. The concepts covered in this course are fundamental, as your project will build with Travis CI only if it contains a valid format using travis.yml.

Azure DevOps

A service to continuously build, test, and deploy to any platform and cloud. You define pipelines and stages of your CI/CD process using YAML.

Azure DevOps provides other options like a visual designer for defining build and release pipelines. However, using YAML offers additional flexibility as you can manage this like any other source file and version control it.

Jenkins X

Jenkins X is an open-source CI/CD automation tool for cloud-native applications on Kubernetes.

YAML plays an essential role in Jenkins X. The Jenkins X cluster configuration process creates YAML based pipeline configuration file called Jenkins-x.yml.

Spring boot

Spring Boot is an open-source Java-based framework used to create a microservice.

Understanding YAML is fundamental if you are developing using Spring Boot. It uses a YAML file called application.yml to store its configuration properties.

Docker

Docker is a set of platforms as a service (PaaS) product that uses OS-level virtualization to deliver software in packages called containers.

Multi-container applications in Docker are defined using a tool called Compose, which uses a YAML file named docker-compose.yml to configure the application's services.

Chef Automate

Chef Automate is an enterprise platform that allows developers, operations, and security engineers to collaborate effortlessly on delivering application & infrastructure changes at the speed of business.

It uses the YAML resource block to declare the configuration data to be tested.

Ansible

Ansible is an open-source software provisioning, configuration management, and application-deployment tool enabling infrastructure as code.

Ansible uses YAML for expressing Ansible playbooks because it is straightforward for humans to understand, read and write compared to other data formats like XML and JSON.

Kubernetes

Kubernetes (known as *k8s*) is an open-source container-orchestration system for automating computer application deployment, scaling, and management.

Kubernetes resources, such as pods, services, and deployments, are created declaratively by using the YAML files.

Swagger

A simple yet powerful tool for RESTful API documentation and design. It is part of the open tools initiative backed by Microsoft, Google, PayPal, and

IBM. Using YAML, you can create a Swagger instance of your API. Swagger consumes specifications in YAML format as input and generates HTML documentation of the API.

And many more...

The details of each tool are beyond this course's scope.

You will find the key concepts covered in this course helpful going forward if you plan to learn or use any of the tools and technologies mentioned above.

Parsing and Emitting YAML

YAML Parsers and Emitters Libraries

and many more...

Figure B-1: YAML Parsers and Emitter Libraries

You would need a YAML parser and emitter library to validate the structural correctness and extract information from a text input in YAML format.

An emitter is a kind of code generator that can convert a native language data type into a YAML format.

- **C - LibYAML** - A C library for parsing and emitting YAML.
- **Python - PyYAML** - YAML parser and emitter for Python
- **Ruby - ruby/yaml** - provides a Ruby interface for data serialization in YAML format.

- **Go - go-yaml** - enables Go programs to encode and decode YAML values comfortably.
- **PHP - symfony/yaml** - It parses YAML strings to convert them to PHP arrays.
- **.NET - YamlDotNet** - .NET library for YAML
- **JavaScript - js-YAML** - YAML parser for JavaScript
- **Java - SnakeYAML Engine** is a YAML 1.2 processor for the Java Virtual Machine version 8 and higher.
- **Perl - [YAML::PP]** is a Perl-based modular YAML processor.

You will find the above helpful list if you want to evaluate various programming languages for their YAML support to build an application consuming and exchanging data in YAML format.

APPENDIX B

Links to Useful YAML Tools

Below are some handy tools you may find convenient while creating or editing a YAML data file using any of the above applications.

- **YAML Lint (http://www.yamllint.com/):** Validate and Verify your documents by pasting your YAML on this page.
- **YAML Validator (https://codebeautify.org/yaml-validator):** Like the YAML lint tool, you can Copy, Paste and Validate your YAML data online with this tool.
- **YAML Beautifier (https://codebeautify.org/yaml-beautifier):** online tool to convert unformatted or ugly YAML data into a well-formatted one for saving and sharing with others.
- **YAML Converter (https://codebeautify.org/yaml-to-json-xml-csv):** convert your YAML data into JSON, XML, or CSV (comma separated values) format online.
- **Online YAML Parser (http://yaml-online-parser.appspot.com/):** write some 'YAML,' and it outputs the corresponding JSON format in real-time.
- **YAML to PDF Table Converter (https://www.beautifyconverter.com/yaml-to-pdf-converter.php):** Online tool to convert YAML to PDF table.

You will find the above helpful list if you want to evaluate various programming languages for their YAML support to build an application that consumes and exchanges data using the YAML format.

APPENDIX C

Where to Go from Here

The book has also been adapted in an interactive course at Educative.io (https://www.educative.io/courses/introduction-to-yaml). Here you would be able to test your skills acquired through code playground in your browser.

 Tarun Telang

Introduction to YAML

Figure C-1: Introduction to YAML (Educative.io)

I have also made an online video course covering the fundamental concepts of this book at skillshare.com. You can watch this course for free by visiting the link below:
(https://www.skillshare.com/r/user/taruntelang?gr_tch_ref=on&gr_trp=on).

If you do not have a skillshare.com subscription, clicking on the above referral link also entitles you to 1 free month of Skillshare.

105 students   35m

Learn YAML from Scratch

Tarun Telang

Figure C-2: Learn YAML from Scratch (Skillshare.com)

Now you can apply these skills to your use cases. I hope you enjoy using YAML as much as I do!

Bibliography

[1] T. Telang, "What is block style in YAML? - educative.io,,"
www.educative.io, [Online]. Available:
https://www.educative.io/answers/what-is-block-style-in-yaml.

Index

www.ingramcontent.com/pod-product-compliance
Lightning Source LLC
La Vergne TN
LVHW051717050326
832903LV00032B/4250